Learn to Play the Rhyming Way

by

Gary Ley BSc (Hons)

This book has been developed as a fun and handy
teaching aid for all Gary's students in order
to reinforce fundamental theories of golf
via humorous rhymes, along with quirky sketches.

Learn to Play the Rhyming Way by Gary Ley BSc (Hons)

© 2012

Cover design: Anabel Temple

Published by House of Pfeffer Limited, 52 Florence Road, Wimbledon, London SW19 8TJ

www.houseofpfeffer.com

All Rights Reserved

First edition

ISBN 978-0-9564525-1-1

Dedication

To my previous & current students, my publishers Michael & Joe, my editor Joe and, of course, my family of girls, Marie; Sam; Isabella; Paloma & Marina who have, in one way or another, kept me on my toes.

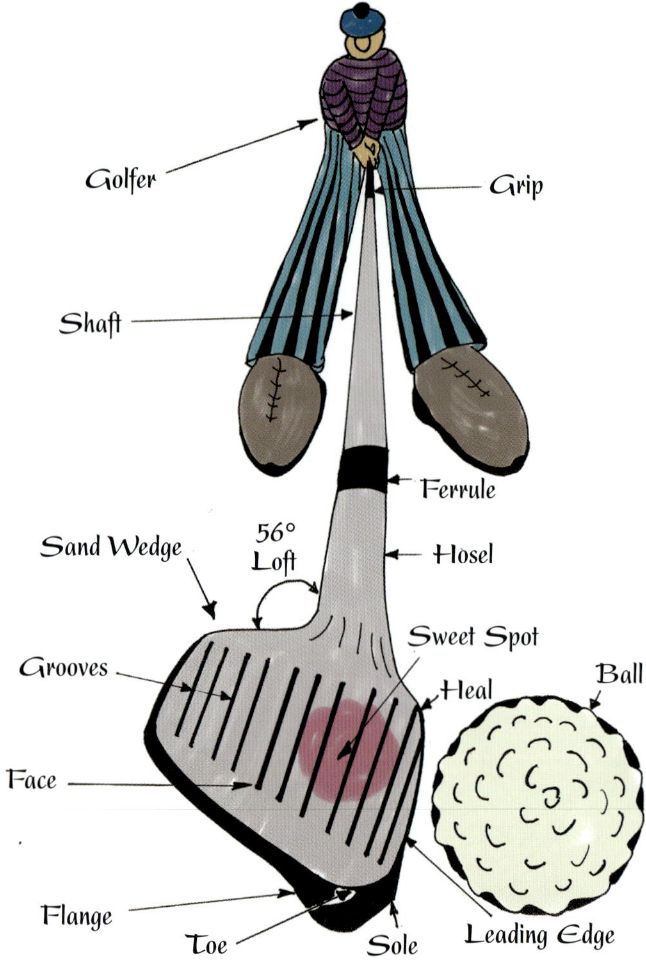
Golfer
Grip
Shaft
Ferrule
56° Loft
Sand Wedge
Hosel
Sweet Spot
Grooves
Heal
Ball
Face
Flange
Toe
Sole
Leading Edge

Contents/index

1. Get a Grip
2. Enhanced Stance
3. Posture Roster
4. The Swing Thing
5. Good Wood
6. Well-Ironed
7. With The Shaped Shot You Have The Lot
8. (a) When Ball Spin Is A Sin
   (b) Controlled Spin Is The Thing
9. Short And Sweet
10. HapHazard
11. Putt Up Or Shut Up
12. Rhythm, No Blues
13. Scoring's Not Boring
14. Stableford Points The Way
15. Concentration Equals Celebration
16. Equipment: And Size Does Matter
17. Dress Code
18. Etiquette & Rules: You Need These Tools
19. The 19th Hole Hobby Or Obsession?

Top Tip! Don't over-tighten or strangle the grip, hold it firmly but gently before letting rip.

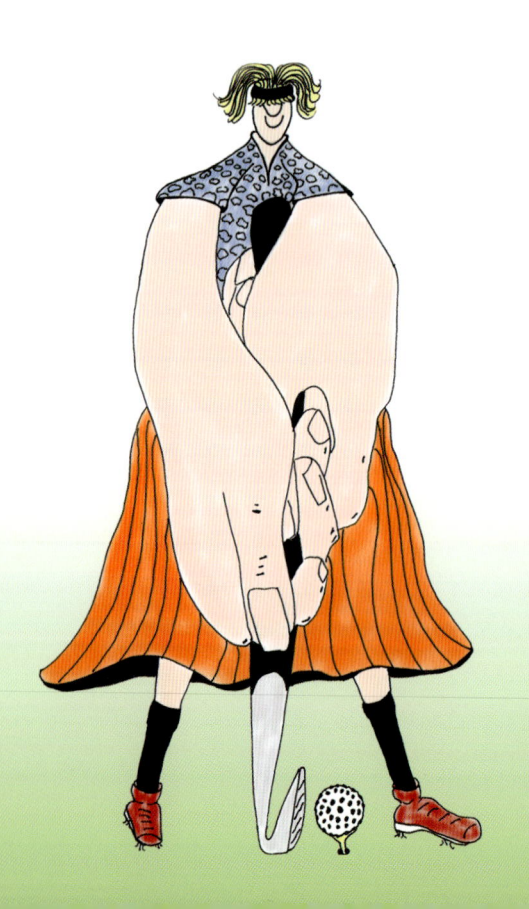

Get a Grip

The best grip for a golfer to use
to ensure the fingers correctly fuse
is the interlocking type
uniting both hands for consistent ball flight

Hold club in front of where you stand
take an under-grip with your left hand

Next is an over-grip with the right
bind together firmly, not too tight

Overlap little finger on right, don't fidget
let it fit over left hand's first digit

When it feels locked over index one
hands and club will move as one.

Enhanced Stance

The real importance of the stance
is like the step to any dance

Legs a bit wider than the hips
same width as the shoulder tips

Knees a touch 'knocked' in
you model the shape of a bowling pin

Once this basic form is found
you're less likely to slam the ground
or get a topping shock up the arm
nasty pins & needles in the palm

You'll soon be hitting it out of the screws
(the old name for wood head grooves).

Top Tip!

When the ball's above stance
choke down on the grip,
'give it some welly'
and turn the hips.

Top Tip! On all slopes, shoulders, hips and knees, parallel to incline gives results that please.

Posture Roster

Body shape remains the same
for almost every aspect of the game

So here's the code to keep it mean
from tee to fairway and on to the green

Place left hand at the base of the spine
bend from hips, 30 degree incline

Relax your arms, first let them dangle
that should give you the proper angle

Unlock and bend those knobbly knees
don't exaggerate the flex, please

Slightly stick out your exterior end
then your set up will be splend-id.

The Swing Thing

It's crucial to settle, relax, be calm
now gently straighten your left arm

Loosen your body don't get too tight
ready, but not rigid, will get to feel right

Look down, and keep looking, at the ball
ease club straight back for a gentle haul
think of it as a pendulum action
up and down rhythmically
or you'll end up in traction

Head still, arms straight, keep knees bent
will help avoid lumbar accident.

Top Tip! Balls that rest on up or downhill lies, must be hit off the back foot, guys.

Top Tip! For fairway shots using hybrid sticks ball set up in middle of stance for the right mix.

Good Wood

We'd all like to crack 300 yards with a driver
regular and smooth like a windscreen wiper
but it's also the most unforgiving club in the bag
bear that in mind when giving it jack-the-lad

The No 1 wood is the master blaster
don't belt it too hard or you'll put someone in plaster

Woods used to be timber, now they're synthetic
the club does the work so don't get frenetic

Let the line of the swing push it up the fairway
don't try to whack it, it'll just go its own way

No need to panic if you're in the light rough
use the 3 or 5 to get clear of the stuff.

Well-Ironed

To judge the distance each club will go
remember these yardages to maintain your flow

3 irons fly 200 yards or more
to carry 190 take out a 4

To achieve 180 a 5 is the stick
if you want 170 then take a 6

So it runs till you're down to 120
when a pitching wedge should be plenty.

Top Tip! For shots in long rough we must state take nothing less than a trusty 8.

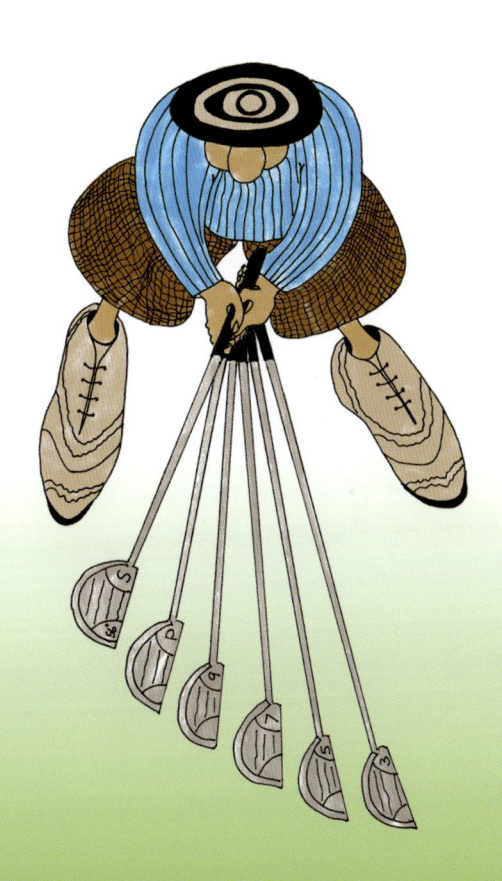

Top Tip! Alignment dictates a ball's trajectory of flight, so from behind the ball view target line, before strike.

1ST TEE
305 YARD
PAR 4
DOGLEG RIGHT

With The Shaped Shot You Have The Lot

To hit a controlled, bended shot
we don't have to change a lot

Just tweak the set-up slightly
in order to be aiming rightly

To achieve a soft, faded flight
club face opens pointing right
with feet aligning to the left
left-to-right fade is what you get

For a draw we do the opposite
which gives a more distance hit
both provide a curving-ball strike
around hazards, trees and the odd rusty bike.

When Ball Spin Is A Sin

When playing into the wind
speeding up the swing is a sin

Taking more club is the thing
and slowing down the swing

Choke-down on the grip a bit
hands ahead of ball when you hit

This keeps the ball flight low
(also gives the grass a mow).

Top Tip!

For chip shots hands ahead of ball,
no need to 'break' the wrists at all.

Top Tip! Cheap, rock-hard power-balls for distance haul, but for spin control use a high grade softer ball.

Controlled Spin Is The Thing

Striking a ball sweetly
imparts backspin neatly

Achieved only off
club face grooves for loft
and club head speed
95 mph does the deed

Ball hit square on
for it to go along
in the air with spin
over pin for backspin.

Short And Sweet

If a hacker wants to make a name
the secret lies in the short game

The real key to the golfer's art
is found in control of the upper-body parts

Thighs, calves and head remain still
shoulders, arms and hands in line for the kill

Head should not rise when taking the shot
this also avoids right shoulder drop
(and a two-foot flop).

Top Tip! For a short chip-and-run shot situation, use a 7 with a putting grip, it's a revelation.

Top Tip! Turning shoulders, hips and knees horizontally around will make sure you stay spinning parallel to the ground.

HapHazard

The wider the stance when nestling in sand
the easier it is to lob it back on land

45 degrees from ball-to-target line
will ensure it pops out first time

Ball in line with your front foot
just inside the heel it has to be put

Open the face of your trusty sand wedge
aiming to hit with the leading edge

2 inches behind the ball to splash it
trying to lift the bugger is bound to hash it.

Putt Up Or Shut Up

Most good putting is about judgement of length
'reading' the green and assessing the 'strength'

A relaxed but firm grip with club 'square' to hole
an easy pendulum action is the sure putter's goal

Get down on your haunches check 'ball-to-hole' line
left eye aligned with ball for a stroke that will shine

(Remember the adage all golfers should know
driving for show, putting for dough).

Top Tip! When in match play putting for a 'half' never leave it short, or you will raise a laugh.

Top Tip! Suck in air to avoid 1st-tee consternation, breathe out during swing to avoid asphyxiation.

Rhythm, No Blues

Golf's a maddening game
of art and craft in a blur
grip, set up, swing and
well-angled shaft (ooh-er)

From tee to green it's not power,
but rhythm, that counts
head and feet still
and consistent swing removes doubts

The best results are achieved
you will find
when bad or good shots
don't faze a cool mind

A smile at your cock-ups
enhances your game
rather than bellowing
a foul-mouthed refrain.

Scoring's Not Boring

There is a need to record all shots
including those flops and tops
on the provided course score card
which reflects all misses and holes parred

Don't forget those unlucky bogies
bet you don't forget the birdies

Carefully record each and every shot
or fellow golfers will soon lose the plot

All above tells if you are on song
at worst, how badly it's coming along

But even better than any of that
it'll give you a certificate for a handicap.

Top Tip! For any out of bounds or lost ball doubt
fire a provisional ball to leave you in with a shout.

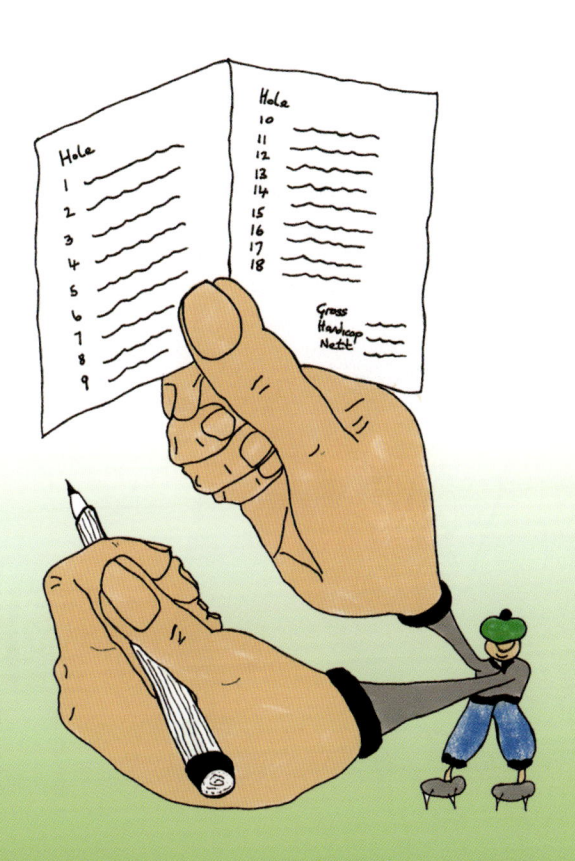

Top Tip! For perfect scoring use a controlled back-swing tempo speed of just one, coupled with a down-swing motion force three times that sum.

Stableford Points The Way

A double bogey gets you none
single bogey saves a 'one'

Par gives you two
punch the air shout yahoo!

Sink a birdie for three, stone me!

Eagle for four, now that's some score

An Albatross for an unlikely five
gets you back in the clubhouse glowing with pride

If you can't manage to score at all
don't waste time just pick up your ball.

15

Concentration Equals Celebration

Regular patterns in your golf approach,
is almost like having an on-course coach

Consistency is an aid to concentration,
takes 'over-thinking' away for true relaxation

The idea is to banish the woes,
but still remain on your toes

This is by far the best way,
to facilitate consistent play

If you bungle your swing, it's no big thing,

When you have a clear mind,
then you've learnt to unwind.

Top Tip!

Golf is a game of the mind, stay in the present through difficult times.

Top Tip! Ball markings should point along target line on the tee or on greens it'll keep your aim fine.

Equipment: And Size Does Matter

Of the woods, irons & putter
only 14, rule books utter

Pencil and tees, you'll need lots of these

A fair size bag, not too big or you'll lag

Towel and brush, to keep equipment plush

Glove on the weaker hand
for grip, not fashion, you understand

Shoes with rubber-type spike
or be told by the captain to take a hike

And last of all…

don't forget your ball.

Dress Code

A golfer really should turn up smart,
it helps to play well if you're looking sharp

Always dress in a shirt with a collar,
makes you look a million dollars

Customarily worn with a sleeve, if you please
trousers to be neat, shorts in the heat,

tailored of course, to avoid being coarse,
and you must wear socks, or be clamped in the stocks.

Top Tip! Do not attempt to hit a ball from water, well not unless you can see at least a quarter.

Top Tip!

If in trouble take a penalty drop shot
if you can't, make sure the shot's hot.

Etiquette & Rules, You Need These Tools

Golf etiquette is often common sense
and does not have to be too intense

For example, just shout 'FORE'
with one almighty ROAR
if a ball's off target at force
towards other players on the course

Another one to watch for, you'll find
is not to stand on a player's putting line

Be aware when others are about to swing
don't move, talk or do anything

All the above refer to general play
but for competitions we must say
purchase a 'Book of Golf Rules'
for any golfer, a vital tool.

Top Tip!

Enjoy your golf, even when things go wrong
don't wallow, let it go, that'll keep you on-song.

The 19th Hole
Hobby or Obsession?

Golf was once for Royals and Toff's
invented by some Scottish boff's

Today it's played by all social strata
as golf catches up with Magna Carta

So what is it about the golf game
that drives those who play insane?

They need to play it day & night
until they get it absolutely right

This hobby is sure to become
an overwhelming obsession for some
an adrenaline rush to better one's self

So, why not try it out yourself.

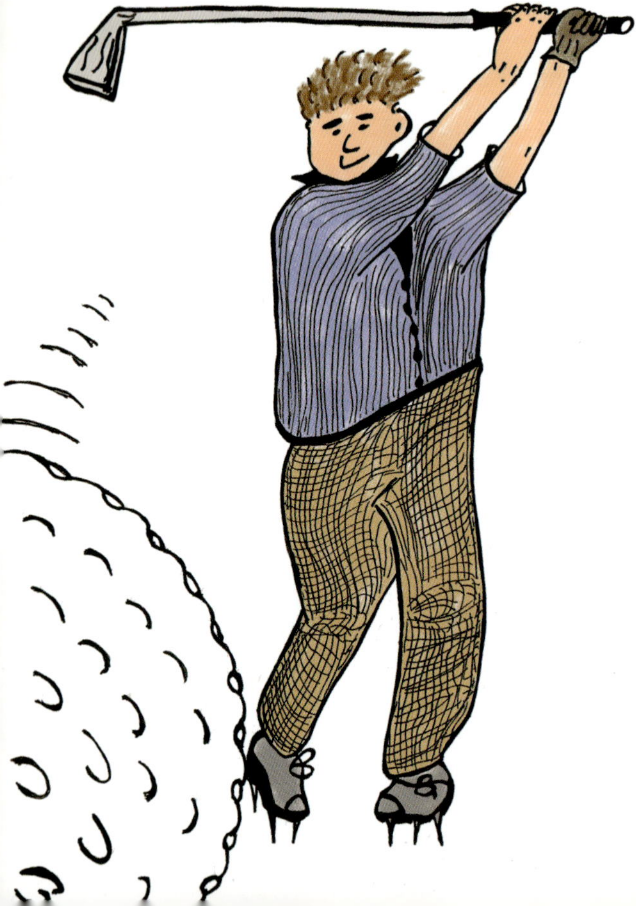

Gary Ley has always had a passion for playing all types of sport along with his other interests of writing, painting and drawing.

Previously, Gary Ley has had one illustrated children's short story book published.

His art work sells successfully in a local art gallery near his home in Richmond upon Thames, Surrey.

Golf and football have played a big part in Gary's life, where he has represented his county in both fields.

Gary is a self-taught golf coach with a strong philosophy that golf should always be made simple, making it joyful and fun to play.

His experience of teaching golf runs at various levels from Special Needs, adults and children of all ages.

Gary is now a golf coach at two London-based Golf Centres where he also manages a very successful Ladies' Academy and Members' Section.

Future titles in ' Learn to play, the Rhyming Way'

Football

Tennis

Cricket

Enquiries at www.houseofpfeffer.com